LIVING IN A FALLEN WORLD

DayOne

HELP!

MY MARRIAGE HAS GROWN COLD

Rick Thomas

Consulting Editor: Dr. Paul Tautges

© Day One Publications 2010

First printed 2010

ISBN 978-1-84625-219-8

All Scripture quotations, unless stated otherwise, are from
the English Standard Version, Crossway, 2001.

Published by Day One Publications
Ryelands Road, Leominster, HR6 8NZ

TEL 01568 613 740 FAX 01568 611 473

email—sales@dayone.co.uk

UK web site—www.dayone.co.uk

USA web site—www.dayonebookstore.com

Designed by **documen**
Printed by Orchard Press (Cheltenham) Ltd

Contents

Contents

As a professional counselor, I find that a large number of counseling issues are marriage-related. Whenever two people choose to live in a one-flesh union for the rest of their lives, there are inevitably and understandably challenging issues that they will have to work through.

The transformation from two independent, self-focused people to a one-flesh, other-centered union is not an easy process. Each person's unique baggage is not checked at the door when he or she enters into the marriage relationship. What a person was prior to marriage, good and bad, is what the person will be during the marriage, unless he or she makes the necessary changes needed in order to live the rest of life in harmony. Participating in a wedding ceremony, making a vow to God, and saying "I do," do not fundamentally change a person from what he or she has always been. Nor do these things release a couple from future problems.

While the dating or courting process can be helpful, it is not a perfect filter to ferret out the good and bad of a person's character, presuppositions, attitudes, and behavior. Truly, there is no perfect system, except the marriage itself, to reveal our true selves. The crucible of marriage is an excellent process that will isolate and identify who two people really are. However, once we learn who we really are, we still need assistance and guidance to help us get from where we are now to where we need to be. The sad news for most marriages is that a struggling couple do not have a "life coach" to guide them through the intricacies of the relationship. They blindly trudge alone through the morass of marriage, not knowing where to turn to when, after a period of neglect, the relationship that began so warmly turns so painfully cold.

This booklet is an attempt to walk through some of the pitfalls of two souls in trouble, while offering practical help in working through specific marriage challenges in a God-glorifying way.

The Bible is my starting point and the filter through which I interpret all of life. As Peter said in 2 Peter 1:3,

His divine power has granted to us all things
that pertain to life and godliness, through the
knowledge of him who called us to his own
glory and excellence.

Therefore, the goal of this book is to apply God's Word practically to two souls in marriage trouble.

This booklet takes the form of a case study of a woman in a marriage that has grown cold. I interact primarily with the woman. However, the teaching presented is not gender-specific. If you are a husband in a marriage that has grown cold, you can easily apply the same truths to your life and marriage. At the end of the booklet I suggest ways to win your unwilling spouse back to the marriage and, more importantly, back to God.

The Case of the Desperate Housewife

Julie[1] was an attractive twenty-eight-year-old Christian who desired to be married. She completed her four-year college degree and landed an outstanding job with a Fortune 500 company. From all perspectives her life was going well. She was young, smart, and on the rise in the corporate world. However, if you talked to Julie she would say that her life was not only incomplete, but was passing her by altogether.

By nature, Julie was not an impulsive person, but from her perspective there was a low-grade discontent in her life. She believed she had done all she was supposed to do at this point, but there was still something missing. Julie wanted to be married. From her perspective, she was ready for the next big

[1] The names of the people in this booklet have been changed, as has certain other information, to protect identities.

step. Unfortunately, there were no eligible candidates in her local church and her current job was not an option as far as finding a godly man she would want to partner with for life.

She told herself, as well as her friends, that she was not desperate, but whether it was in her own mind or in the conversations with her girlfriends, the topics of marriage and singleness always seemed to come up. Occasionally, others would tell Julie that she seemed to be fixated on marriage. Julie would dismiss their observations as untrue. It wasn't that Julie could not see their point, but she refused to acknowledge that the issue was to her as big as they were saying it was. In her heart of hearts, however, she intuitively knew that their assessment was true.

She later said, "When I was single, I felt as though I was in a prison, though I would rarely be honest with myself because I knew it was temporary and there was hope that I would be released some day. And in time I met Bob. We fell in love and eventually got married. Now here I am, five years into our marriage, and I have no clue what really happened. Truthfully, it feels that all I've done is switch prisons. I jumped from the frying pan of singleness into the fire of marriage. There is one big difference, however. The prison of singleness had an ending, while the prison of marriage appears to have no hope of ever ending. What can I do?"

Bob seemed to be an answer to prayer when they first met. He was a nice, well-mannered, and likable guy who was a ministry leader in his local church. He seemed to be perfect. His pastor was the one who introduced Bob to Julie. After their first year of marriage, however, what appeared to be a good catch was looking more like a bad trap.

Bob had conveniently failed to mention to any of his friends or his future wife his addiction to porn. Within the first six months of their marriage Julie found some pornography links from a history check on Bob's computer. In addition, it became apparent that, while Bob had many ministry friends, he had no real close friends in his life. Everyone seemed to know Bob, but no one really knew Bob. He was adept at keeping people out of his life—until he married Julie.

Julie thought she could confront Bob about the pornography, but when she did, he responded with rage, accusations, and threats that if she ever told anyone about the porn, their marriage would be over. She was now afraid to say anything to anyone.

Julie turned up for counseling. Bob was resistant to her going but finally relented. He did say that it would be a "cold day" before he ever went to a counselor. Julie knew that if her marriage was going to survive, she would have to do the heavy lifting, at least in the beginning.

Julie's Lonely Journey Begins

> And we know that for those who love God
> all things work together for good, for those
> who are called according to his purpose.
> (Romans 8:28)

After a couple of sessions of getting to know Julie, I began to ask her specific questions regarding her basic understanding of theology and how that theology worked out practically in her life. I knew that, if I could uncover what she believed about God and how she applied her understanding of God to her life, I would then be at a starting point in understanding how she had gotten to this place. The answer to every issue that she would ever encounter, including her current marriage problems, would, in the final analysis, flow out of her theology: specifically, how she thought about God, and how she practically applied those thoughts to her life.

I discovered that Julie's core theology was wrapped

up in her misunderstanding of the word "good." She came to realize that her understanding of and desire for what is good were different from what the Bible portrays as good.

While all things do work together for "good" for the Christian, according to the teaching of Paul in Romans 8:28, the reality of that text for Julie was frustrating. Sadly, she had misinterpreted Paul's meaning. One of the first things I did was assess and adjust her interpretation and expectation of what "good" meant to her. She had been set on a course to find and experience good for many years. And it was very clear that she had a simplistic and incomplete idea of what "good" meant from a theological perspective.

In order to explore this with her, I had to get her to think through what Paul was thinking in Romans 8:28, and how Paul wanted us to interpret the "good" that happens to us when trouble comes. Most certainly, the "good" does not necessarily mean that I will live a healthy, wealthy, and peaceful life. It also does not mean that, when trouble comes, God is about to turn this tragedy or disappointment into some kind of man-centered prosperity or preferred outcome for me.

Let me illustrate this with the story of Debra.

Debra was in an automobile accident and her car was completely wrecked. Through the ordeal, she received an incredible insurance claim that allowed her to buy a car that was far better than her previous, aging vehicle. Though God did work these things into her life and she did receive a brand-new vehicle, it can be misleading to bring Romans 8:28 to bear on this situation. For some, it might imply that God is our "Divine Dreamweaver." This is not the "good" that Paul was talking about.

Whether or not your life and circumstances unfold to your liking is not the point of the Bible and neither is it the point of your life. Giving you the life you've always wanted is not at the top of God's "to do" list.

▶ Jesus's life ended in death so that God could bring about good. This is the ultimate Good News (Hebrews 2:14–15)!

▶ Joseph's life landed him in a pit and then a prison in order to bring about good (Genesis 50:20).

▶ Moses spent forty years in a desert to bring about good (Acts 7:20–35).

▶ Esther was willing to lay down her life to bring about good (Esther 4:16).

▶   Job lost everything, but from his horrible experience came good (Job 42:10).

The good that God is working in me and you is to make us more like Jesus. If the circumstances in my world are not conforming me to Jesus, I'm missing the point of what is going on in my life.

The point of the Bible is transformation, not seven habits for highly effective people. Neither is it my personal success or happiness as defined by our culture. If I gain personal property, acclaim, or significant monetary worth in this life, but these means of prosperity do not conform me to the image of God's Son, I have missed the point of God's work in my life.

The "good" in Romans 8:28, and the point of the whole passage, is that I will be changed into the image of Christ, but will not necessarily grow healthy, wealthy, and wise.

> And we know that for those who love God
> all things work together for good, for those
> who are called according to his purpose.
> For those whom he foreknew he also
> predestined to be conformed to the image
> of his Son, in order that he might be the

firstborn among many brothers. And those
whom he predestined he also called, and
those whom he called he also justified, and
those whom he justified he also glorified.

(Romans 8:28–30)

During my counseling sessions with Julie it became apparent that she saw her marriage as something to be desired in order to bring about her personal interpretation of what is good. The trap that Julie fell into was a trap of her own making. Her hope, after her marriage had grown cold, was for her husband to change. While Bob did need to change, the first order of business, as it pertained to Julie, was for her to change. Her theology and practice of theology needed to be reshaped before she could address the obvious flaws in Bob and their marriage.

The Snare of Perceived Needs

One of the more obvious traps that Julie had fallen into was that her desire for marriage and companionship had morphed into something that God never intended. She had gotten herself caught up in the self-centered craving for getting her perceived needs met, as popularized by our Christian culture.

She saw the "good" that God offered her through the lens of contemporary Christian literature rather than through the lens of Scripture.

"Love Languages," "Love and Respect," "His Needs, Her Needs": these are some of the books and buzzwords that are bandied about in Christendom in an effort to resolve relational conflict. While I understand why such materials exist, these concepts are, in marriage counseling specifically, generally more of a hindrance than a help. This kind of thinking has most assuredly been a hindrance for Julie. If Julie had a right understanding of God and his gospel, her approach would have been more like the Savior's, which was characterized by serving rather than seeking to be served:

> For even the Son of Man came not to be
> served but to serve, and to give his life as a
> ransom for many.
>
> (Mark 10:45)

Rarely do counselees talk this way. They do not see the necessity of first restoring their relationship with God. This was a huge element missing in Julie's thinking. She seemed not to understand that her sinful attitudes toward Bob, as well as her desire for

Bob to meet her "needs," had grieved God and had in part set the marriage up for failure. The weight of the marriage failure was not entirely her fault, but she was the one who had sought counseling and, at that time, the only one I could counsel.

Julie's main concerns were that her husband had not been meeting her needs or speaking her "love language." She also had a list of ideas of how he could speak her love language in more practical ways. Later, upon further exploration with Bob, I learned that he was frustrated because his wife did not respect him. He had ideas in his mind of what his love for her could look like if only she would make the first move by meeting his needs.

Each spouse had been manipulating the other, while neither was grieved over how they had been dishonoring God. Their relationship was more about mutual need-meeting than confessing their personal sin against God. If they chose to restore their broken relationship with God, then they would be well on their way to restoring their broken relationship with each other.

Any Christian spouse can get the love he or she desires. But it cannot be found through self-centered or self-serving methods. To skip or marginalize God in order to have a great marriage is like trying to have a wonderful meal without food. It is incoherent. When a spouse understands the gospel rightly, he or she will see how the gospel is not about getting needs met, but about pursuing one another in love.

The reason I love Christ so much is because he unselfishly came to this planet to rescue me from my sin. He saved me and now he is restoring me to himself. One day he will allow me to join him in heaven to live an eternal existence with him. He accomplished this by taking on human flesh, living three decades on earth, and then dying on the cross. God poured out his wrath on Christ while he was hanging on that cross. Christ took my place. This is the gospel. It is unfathomable, stunning love. It is this kindness that bends my heart toward Christ in repentance.

> ... do you presume on the riches of his
> kindness and forbearance and patience, not
> knowing that God's kindness is meant to
> lead you to repentance?
>
> (Romans 2:4)

How nice it would be if we could dismiss the Christian "mutual need-meeting" ideas and seek practically to be kind to one another the way Christ has been kind to us, as motivated by and understood through the cross. Rather than trying to figure out our "languages," we can die to self and aggressively love others. In God's economy we receive by giving, not the other way around. This is what Paul was saying in Ephesians 5:27:

> ... so that he might present the church to
> himself in splendor, without spot or wrinkle
> or any such thing, that she might be holy
> and without blemish.

Christ will receive what he paid and worked for: a church in all her splendor. A husband who chooses to die to his desires and seeks to serve his wife will receive a special kind of lady. A wife who chooses to do the same for her husband will be well on her way to enjoying a much better marriage.

However, it is true that there are real specific needs that must be met. As I have pondered this "need" question over the years, I have come up with my personal list of needs. I believe this list is exhaustive.

▶ Physical needs: air, water, shelter, food, health
▶ Spiritual needs: God's salvation and ongoing
   Spirit empowerment

In counseling, however, it is a different story. Over

19

the years I have heard person after person give me a laundry list of all their needs. Here are some of the front-runners:

▶ Love

▶ Sex

▶ Communication

▶ Companionship

▶ Significance

▶ Acceptance

▶ Respect

I think that, in most cases, the counselees do not realize what they are saying when they say they have a need outside the real needs I listed above. Furthermore, they do not realize how their craving for a particular "need" is controlling them.

Often I will illustrate the difference between a need and desire this way:

"If you held me underwater in a swimming pool, I would fight you to the end because I need air. A need is something you cannot live without. But when you elevate desires to the level of needs, there is some form of idolatry going on, and if you don't repent of your

idolatry, that craving will wreck the relationship from which you are trying to extract that perceived need."

Love Is All I Need!

A common rebuttal to the "need theory" concepts is that we need love. What we really need, however, is a relationship with God; if we have that, and the relationship is right, our demands on other humans to meet our cravings for love should not be controlling. *If you are resting in the gospel, you can turn the tables on all your relationships; rather than being a deficient taker, you can be an abundant giver.* Rather than expecting others to meet your inordinate craving for love, you will be able to love others. You will be Christlike. He did not come here to be loved, but to serve (see Mark 10:45).

Imagine if Christ had said, "I need love. These people are not respecting me. I'm not feeling accepted today. I'm feeling a bit rejected, and it is not right. My craving for love is not being met and therefore I must do something to bend their good favor toward me. My feelings are hurt and I'm getting angry with these people who seem determined not to meet my needs."

Christ was so connected to his Father that he

was not controlled by the hurtful opinions or the disappointing acts of others. He was not on the defensive while responding to others; he was on the offensive. He set himself to give love, rather than waiting for someone to meet his needs. He was not controlled by others, because he knew his purpose in life, what he came to do, and which relationship really mattered. He was led and loved by his Father, therefore he was not controlled by the whims of people.

Years ago I heard Christian author and speaker Paul Tripp present a five-step analysis of what happens when a person distorts and twists desires into needs:

1. Desire: "You should do _____ for me."

2. Need: "You will do _____ for me."

3. Expectation: "I expect you to do _____ for me."

4. Disappointment: "You didn't do_____ for me."

5. Punishment: "You didn't do _____ for me, so I am going to make you pay in some way."

Whenever our desires or cravings morph into needs, we can expect this downward spiral to result in a sinful confrontation.

Julie's life and thoughts had been more about

what she wanted than what God wanted. God was just one of the options she used to bring her what she wanted. Her theology and understanding of God were twisted. For Julie, Bob was another means to feel good about herself. Sadly for Julie, she married a selfish person. Bob was not compliant in meeting her perceived needs. And when Bob was not compliant, Julie became angry, critical, sad, self-pitying, and unloving toward Bob. This selfish, reciprocal interaction caused them to inch gradually away from each other until their home was too divided for the problem to be ignored any longer.

While Bob was not right in his selfish attitudes and responses to his wife, Julie needed to readjust her thinking into a God-centered way of looking at things, rather than a Julie-centered way.

Bringing the Gospel to Bear on a Marriage Grown Cold

After I had helped Julie unpack her thoughts and her heart's motivations, and walked her through her understanding of God and how she had been selfishly relating to God, I began to explore in a deeper way the implications and applications of the gospel. Initially, Julie was not satisfied with this approach to counseling. She wanted what she called "real" and "practical" ideas and methods that she could immediately apply to her life. Talking about the gospel at that early point in the counseling was counter-intuitive. Even though Julie had spent twenty years thinking wrongly about God and marriage, she wanted me to fix her marriage immediately. The gospel approach to counseling made no sense to her.

When I raised the gospel as our starting point and the solution to her problems, she told me that she understood the gospel. She said she became a Christian over two decades beforehand. And, on one level, she was telling me the truth. She did understand the gospel, but only as it pertained to her salvation.

I, however, was talking about the gospel as it pertained to sanctification (the life a person lives as he or she is gradually transformed into Christlikeness), though I never want to assume that a person is a Christian. Julie seemed to be a Christian, but she had a limited understanding of how the gospel should rule her life. She believed that she needed the gospel to get saved, but that it had little to no effect on her life after salvation. She did not understand the biblical model, which teaches that we need the gospel for both salvation and sanctification.

What is the Gospel?

The best word to use to describe the gospel is "Jesus." Jesus is the gospel; the gospel is Jesus. When I asked Julie what the gospel was, she said it was the Good News. Though this is right in one sense, she did not fully understand the gospel as a person. The gospel for her was more about the proclamation of a message than about a transformative way to live. The gospel is not just a proclamation, it is a person! The person is Jesus.

We can expand this succinct definition this way: The gospel is the *Person* and *work* (everything he has done) of Jesus Christ. Christ and his work go back to eternity past, and his Person and activity stretch into everything he will do in eternity future. The centerpieces of all this activity are the cross, where Jesus paid for our sins with his death, and the tomb, from out of which he was raised from the dead.

Once Julie had this understanding of the gospel, I began to walk her through what her response to it and to Christ should be.

The gospel is God's most extravagant outpouring of his love to the world. There is nothing more profound that the Father could have done to prove his love to us than execute his Son on the cross. The gospel is God's final and most complete answer to the question, "Is God good?"

He is good. He is profoundly good.

Unfortunately, though Julie told me that God is good, there was an objective disconnect between what she knew to be true and how she lived that truth out in her life. She did not "marinate" her mind in the gospel, in God's goodness to her specifically. She had not consistently lived in the good of the gospel. Her affection for Christ had been sporadic during the good seasons and non-existent during the bad.

What Is My God Like?

Because Julie did not have a right understanding of the gospel, or an appreciation for it, she had a weak view of God, particularly of his goodness. She had not experienced God's goodness on a daily basis because of her "gospel-disconnect." This had led her to find her own version of goodness. Rather than trusting and resting in the awareness that God is good, she trusted in her ability to find what she thought was good. That led her to make an unwise decision. The concern now was that she would make another unwise decision in her endless craving for what she believed to be good. My goal was to reorient her way of thinking about God and to teach her how to live out this new way of thinking in her everyday life.

A number of years ago, when teaching in a church meeting, I gave an illustration that involved using my then two-year-old son as the prop. The illustration was not rehearsed and my son had no idea he was going to be the day's illustration. I placed him on the table at the front of the room. I then stepped away from him and the table and asked him to jump into my arms. He did, and I caught him. I placed him back on the table and asked him to jump again. He did, and again I caught him. He exercised faith in his daddy.

▶ My son knows who I am.

▶ My son has experienced goodness from me.

▶ My son was willing to trust me, based on his understanding and experience of me.

Using this analogy to think about my relationship to God, I can say:

▶ *Theology* gives me a basic understanding of who my heavenly Father is.

▶ *The gospel* communicates to me, in a profound way, the goodness of my Father.

▶ *Faith* is my willingness to trust my Father during a time of testing, based on my understanding (theology) and experience (gospel) of him.

What if my son had not exercised faith and not jumped into my arms? I would then have been compelled to ask the "why" question: "Haydn, why didn't you have faith in your father?" The answer to that question could be threefold.

▶ Haydn would not exercise faith in me if he was angry with me.

▶ Haydn would not exercise faith in me if he was afraid of me.

▶ Haydn would not exercise faith in me if he was ignorant of me.

This describes Julie's core problem: she tended to fear more than trust. And when fear was ruling her heart, she would not exercise faith in God, but chose to take matters into her own hands. This pattern became more and more obvious as I began to probe her with more questions about other issues in her life. You could paraphrase Julie's thoughts this way:

"I do not understand what God is up to all the time. Sometimes I wonder if he is really good. When I get like this I tend to default to my understanding of what good is by taking matters into my own hands. God won't come through, but I can."

If my son had not trusted me and had chosen to stay on the table, he would have been relying on his own understanding of and solution to the problem at hand. The table he was standing on was what he had faith in. The scary thing for him would be a leap into his daddy's arms. The choice to do it his own way would, therefore, have been a decision to rely on his own sufficiency, rather than his father's.

Dealing with Common Faith-Killers

From this grounded assumption I began to explore with Julie the reason why she had a lack of faith in God. Firstly, she had to understand that Bob was an important, but secondary, issue. While I didn't want to diminish his role in the chaos of the marriage, Julie had to know that the main problem was her longstanding, diminutive relationship with God. Julie's sin pattern of self-sufficiency had been a dominating issue in her life. Her self-sufficiency manifested itself when she chose not to trust God at a particular moment. She preferred to take matters into her own hands, control the situation, and make the decision that suited her personal craving. This is what happened when she and Bob were courting. They had dated for two years. There were signs that things were not right, but at twenty-eight she felt it was too late to start over again. Here was part of her reasoning:

▶ she wasn't sure how long it would take to find another guy;

▶ she wasn't sure if there would ever be
   another guy;

▶ she didn't want to wait to find another guy and
   go through the dating process again;

▶ she was also concerned about what others would
   think. "Why break up with Bob?" they would
   say. "You make such a cute couple."

She later said, "Even as I was walking down the
aisle, looking at Bob, I knew he was not the right
guy. But what was I to do after the waiting, the two
years of dating, the plans for the wedding, and the
expectations from friends and family? Though I was
not at peace about it, I felt God would make it right.
He hasn't, and I'm pretty upset about it."

She chose her version of good rather than trusting
God's good. This choice of hers spoke more about an
issue between her and God than anything else. This
is what I explored. There was something about God
she did not care for, or was not satisfied with. This
is what had led to a diminutive faith. She had been
unwilling to "jump into her daddy's arms" and let
him make the decision.

Here are the three primary reasons I mentioned
above as to why Julie had been unwilling to exercise
full faith in God.

FEAR

At some level in her soul, she was afraid of God. She thought that, if she made a commitment to follow him regardless of what it cost or where it might take her, she might not get what she really wanted. She believed that if she fully trusted God, he would take her further than she'd ever want to go and ask her to do more than she'd ever want to do. Therefore, she generally chose not to trust God, especially when the immediate outlook seemed bad.

In C. S. Lewis's book *The Lion, the Witch and the Wardrobe*, there is a conversation between the Beavers and Lucy about Aslan, the picture of Christ in the book. The conversation goes like this, as Lucy asks, "Then he isn't safe?" Mr. Beaver says, "Safe? Who said anything about safe? Course he isn't safe. But he's good. He's the King, I tell you."[2]

Julie intuitively knew that God was not safe and, therefore, she chose to take matters into her own self-sufficient hands because her personal good was at stake.

ANGER

When Julie was asked about anger toward God, she replied disdainfully that she could never be angry with

2 C. S. Lewis, *The Lion, the Witch and the Wardrobe* (New York: Collier Books, 1975), 75–76.

God. When the matter was explored a bit more, she relented, realizing that maybe she was angry with God.

When most Christians hear the word "anger" they think of explosions. However, most Christians do not struggle this way. Some do, but most do not. The anger I was talking to her about was a "low-grade fever" anger that ran just under the surface of her life and only manifested itself during times of intense tension.

By this kind of anger I am referring to something like disappointment with God. Other "anger words" that made up Julie's personality were frustration, impatience, bitterness, discouragement, and unkindness.

Julie was too Christianized to say she was annoyed with God, but with more reflection she did admit she was quite disappointed that when she was twenty-eight she was still not married. In her mind, God did not come through for her. Therefore, Julie did it her way.

IGNORANCE

This word is not meant in a pejorative way, but to indicate a lack of knowledge or an unawareness of certain things about God. Due to a lack of proper discipleship Julie had come to some very poor conclusions about God.

After a couple of hours' counseling, it became clear that Julie was struggling, at different levels, with all three of these faith-killers. She began to see why she was unwilling to wait and trust God and would rather choose to take matters into her own hands. Julie had become angry and bitter toward God and Bob. Unwittingly, in her heart she had moved from a sense of her personal responsibility in the marriage to a subtle belief that God and Bob had wronged her.

Embracing
the Crucible
of Suffering

Julie had had an idea of what marriage should be like. After several years with Bob, however, her dream had been shattered. She honestly blurted out during one of our sessions, "This is not what I signed up for!"

In his book *A Praying Life*, Paul Miller said, "[Our culture] shapes our responses to the world, and we find ourselves demanding a pain-free life. Our can-do attitude is turning into relentless self-centeredness."[3] Julie had drifted so far from the gospel that she believed she deserved better than all that she had. The Bible tells us that we all deserve hell, and anything better than hell is a plus. Because Julie was a Christian, she was doing far better than she deserved, but she wanted more. Unfortunately for Julie, she had fallen into the American Christian

3 Paul Miller, *A Praying Life* (Colorado: NavPress, 2009), 82.

attitude-trap that does not accommodate suffering.

Listen to the apostle Paul:

> For it has been granted to you that for the
> sake of Christ you should not only believe
> in him but also suffer for his sake.
> (Philippians 1:29)

You won't hear Philippians 1:29 in your "You Want to Become a Christian?" class. Paul says that there are two gifts at salvation: the first is faith in Christ, and the second is personal suffering. God gives you not only the gift of salvation, but also the gift of suffering.

The apostle Peter said it another way:

> For to this you have been called, because
> Christ also suffered for you, leaving you
> an example, so that you might follow in
> his steps.   (1 Peter 2:21)

Typically, when people talk about their calling, they do not reference this passage. Paul was clear; Peter was clear; suffering is part of our calling.

Peter followed his "theology of suffering" passage (1 Peter 2:18–25) with the conjunction "likewise." A conjunction, grammatically, *joins two thoughts.* Peter was joining what he had just said about suffering to his instructions to wives who have husbands who are unresponsive to God (3:1–6).

> Likewise, wives, be subject to your own
> husbands, so that even if some do not obey
> the word, they may be won without a word
> by the conduct of their wives, when they see
> your respectful and pure conduct.
>
> (verses 1–2)

Peter brings a New Testament theological view of suffering into our postmodern living rooms. Julie needed to come to terms with the Christian's view of suffering. Before I could effectively address Bob's issues, Julie had to come to a place of humble repentance.

"What if My Spouse Will Not Repent?"

When a marriage grows cold and only one spouse is willing to work on it, that spouse will have to juxtapose two biblical responsibilities: how to be free in Christ, and how to live in a prison of marriage. Paul said in Philippians 1:12, as he was reflecting upon his own prison sentence,

> *I want you to know, brothers, that what*
> *has happened to me has really served to*
> *advance the gospel.*

I wanted to relate to Julie from more than just a Bible-verse-dispensing mode. Her marriage was a restoration process that called for compassion and patience. Additionally, it was essential that I had a firm grip on the gospel. I needed to understand not only the gospel, but also how the gospel applied practically to her situation. Julie needed to know that she could walk in the Savior's steps with supernatural joy, regardless of the future state of her marriage.

The challenging part was to bring her to a place of change, or what the Bible calls "repentance." It was analogous to coming upon a car wreck in the intersection and asking the one who was most injured why he or she had made a wrong turn. While extending grace, hope, and compassion to Julie, I was clear and practical on how she could get a new-found freedom in Christ. Of course, the freedom I was offering was a freedom that also meant she would stay in her marriage.

Modeling Gospel Attitudes

If you live in such a way that the gospel is *the* reason why you do what you do, you are well on your way to a right understanding and application of Christ in your life. This is what I call *living in the good of the gospel.* The following are some examples of how Jesus is the only right answer for "why" we do what we do. If these ten sample behaviors are motivated by the gospel, the person modeling them is enjoying and benefiting from the gospel. As Julie began to come to terms with the gospel, her heart was more and more shaped by Christ, and these attitudes and behaviors became hers.

1. The gospel is the reason you serve your spouse.

2. The gospel is the reason you ask your son or daughter to forgive you.

3. The gospel is the reason you forgive others.

4. The gospel is the reason you work at your job for the glory of God.

5. The gospel is the reason you think the best about others rather than suspect the worst.

6. The gospel is the reason you ask more questions

rather than make more accusations when confused about a situation.

7. The gospel is the reason you are regularly seeking someone to encourage.

8. The gospel is the reason you befriend people who will speak honestly to you about your life.

9. The gospel is the reason you can't wait to serve someone.

10. The gospel is the reason you express so much gratitude to others.

Julie began to model these gospel attitudes in her life. Rather than running from God by choosing her own way, Julie began to recognize how God was working in her even during her times of suffering. She began to see personal suffering not so much as something happening *to* her, but as something God was doing *in* her.

A right understanding of suffering was a huge thing for Julie to acknowledge. She had positioned herself to understand and embrace her marriage problems because of her growing awareness and application of the gospel to her personal life. Acknowledging that God was doing something in her was more than a courtesy nod or "wave of the hand." It was sobering.

She now knew that God had chosen to work in her, and that understanding humbled her to think that he would take an interest in her. At times she admitted that this new awareness and acceptance of who God really is was frightening (see Job 23:15).

Often in our suffering, we focus on the wrong question. We can be more concerned about whether God is safe than whether he is good. Sometimes our craving for self-protection can trump his good work in our lives. The cross of Christ is the most profound testimony of the safe/good dynamic. The Jews saw the cross as a stumbling block, while the Greeks saw it as foolishness. From God's perspective, the cross was wisdom and power (see 1 Corinthians 1:18–25).

There are times in our lives when what is best for us is not necessarily the *safest* path for us. In those moments, we must understand and believe that God is good and he is working good in us. Like the baker kneading the dough, our great God is working his desires into us to make us vessels fit for his use.

When your time comes to enter the crucible of suffering, remember that God is working for your good. Make copious mental notes of what he is doing in you. Remember the pain. Embrace the suffering. By embracing the suffering, you are embracing the God who is working the suffering into your life.

Though Christ asked for the cup to be taken away from him in the Garden of Gethsemane, ultimately he embraced the Father's work in his life when he said, "not my will, but yours, be done" (Luke 22:42).

Jesus submitted to his Father, even though it meant he would die. He believed in the good purposes of the Father. When we stop resisting our Father's work in our lives and start believing in him, there is hope for change in us. However, to accept the crucible of suffering in your life does not mean your adversity will pass. As in Julie's case, it simply meant she was going to trust the steady hand of God, who was working for her good, regardless of the consequences.

Trusting God does not mean things will turn out the way you had hoped. Christ embraced the will of the Father and was later crucified on the cross. Joseph embraced God's will and his life involved one disappointment after another. Job said,

> *Though he slay me, I will hope in him.*
> (Job 13:15)

Paul believed God and was beheaded. Peter followed his Savior to his own crucifixion.

Trusting God during our times of adversity reveals

a desire to know and follow God regardless of where the path may lead. But we can be assured of this one thing: God is good, because the gospel says he is good. Though you may not know the outcome of God's good work in your life, you can be assured that you will be more than satisfied by relinquishing your rights to him.

God is Already There Before You Get There

I have a friend who lived in open adultery for eighteen years. He was not a Christian and was not shy about his lifestyle. His wife, like Julie, knew most of his sin. My friend's wife chose to honor God by staying in the marriage. It was supernatural. My friend repented of his sin in June 1988. Since that time he has faithfully loved and served his family in the context of a local church. The story of my friend is analogous to Bob and Julie's story. Julie had to confront her own soul about the long-term effects of her present difficulty. She chose to meet God in the crucible of suffering, knowing that he was with her through thick and thin.

These two stories remind me of the story of Joseph in the Old Testament. Though his family was in disarray, Joseph knew that God was not only with him, but also working for Joseph's good.

After the story of Joseph's life finished at the end of Genesis, Moses opened the next book, Exodus, with this tidbit:

> *All the descendants of Jacob were seventy persons; Joseph was already in Egypt.*
> (Exodus 1:5)

Whether or not you know where you are going, there is an abiding truth that is universal and applicable to every person: regardless of your destination, before you get there, you can know, rest, and trust in the fact that God is already there. You cannot go anywhere in life where God is not waiting for you to get there. It is impossible to go ahead of him or to step out of his plans for you. In good times and bad, know that God is ahead of you, waiting on you and ready to take care of you.

As the book of Exodus opens we learn that God had already disrupted the nation of Israel. The Israelites were aware that things had changed in their homeland. There was turmoil. They were in dire straits. The famine had spread beyond normal discomfort and families were struggling to make ends meet. Then God uprooted them and sent them to Egypt.

45

From their initial perspective, there was little hope for change of circumstances. It was not exactly clear what they should do to resolve their problems. From their limited understanding they had no idea of the plans God had made for them. They could only see trouble in their present situation.

In the early verses of Exodus 1 the writer tells us that the Israelites left their homes and headed to an unknown place, Egypt. Though the text does not say it, I'm sure some of them struggled with the disruption of their homes. They were made uncomfortable, and most certainly some would have wavered in their faith about these upheavals.

- Have you ever had an experience when God rearranged the circumstances of your life?

- Have you ever stood at a point when all options seemed to be lined with personal suffering and hardship?

If so, you can understand something of what the children of Israel were going through. They were leaving all they knew. This was a total lifestyle change. People, places, and things were being completely disrupted and there was nothing they could do about it. They were being moved to another place by difficult circumstances.

It is in this context that the writer inserts five little words into the text: "Joseph was already in Egypt"! The meaning is more profound than just letting the other Israelites know where their relative was located. Most certainly, they found Joseph, and his new home in Egypt became their new home.

But the significance of the words is much more than that. This story is also about the *how* and the *why* of Joseph's being in Egypt. As you begin to unpack Joseph's prior circumstances, troubles, and journey to Egypt, you realize that something bigger than suffering was going on here. Then as you read about his rise to prominence and the ensuing famine in the land and the disruption of an entire nation, you begin to get a glimpse of God's kindness to his people through their personal suffering.

▶ Can you see God's kindness through your suffering?

▶ Are you aware that God is ahead of you?

▶ Do you know that your Father cares deeply for you, and that none of his plans for you will be overturned?

47

It took the Israelites a long time to realize that Joseph's relocation to Egypt was orchestrated by the divine and loving hand of God. Regardless of your situation, I can most assuredly tell you that God is already there! Though Bob is still in the process of change, and Julie's marriage is not all she would like it to be, Julie is doing well today, loving and trusting her God while serving him and her husband. God is with her.

During the six months I worked with Julie I began to reorient her life toward a God-centered way of thinking and living. Here are a few ways I helped her through this process.

Gospel

Julie needed to be "gospelized" on a daily basis. Each day she had to "marinate" her mind in the Good News, in the Person and work of Christ. She had to know that God was for her, and the starting and sustaining place for this understanding and practice is the gospel. In Romans 8:31–39 Paul tells us how the gospel is our anchoring hope in times of confusion and despair.

The following are a few suggestions I passed on to Julie and recommend to you in order that you too may anchor yourself in the gospel.

1. Practice praying throughout your day, with an emphasis on gratitude for God's victory on the cross. Thank God for things he brings to your mind throughout the day. Eventually, you'll have a heart of gratitude and a mind that is growing in awareness of all that God is doing in your life.

2. Listen to gospel-centered music.[4] Music is a great way to create emotion. Let your cross-centered thinking affect your emotions. Have the cross stir your emotions.

3. Socialize with gospel-centered friends. As you pray for friends who understand the gospel, begin engaging them by asking them how they apply the gospel to their lives. Ask them to be specific and practical.

4. Read gospel-centered materials.[5] Let gospel-centered authors speak into your life. See the section "Where Can I Get Further Help?" at the end of this booklet for a short "starter list" of gospel-centered materials that can serve you.

4 See "Excellent Worship Music," at Counseling Solutions: competentcounseling.com/2009/07/14/excellent-worship-music/.
5 See "Recommended Books," at Counseling Solutions: competentcounseling.com/distance-education/books-to-read/.

Repentance

Julie needed to repent of her sin. There has never been a bad marriage where one partner was innocent. Since Adam and Eve unraveled into a chaotic mess in the Garden of Eden, every marriage has had two participating sinners who have sinned against each other. No one is free from sin. I had Julie list her sinful attitudes and actions and repent in the appropriate ways the Bible teaches.

I recommend you do the same. Make a "sin list" of every way in which you sin on a regular basis. Enlist a friend who knows and loves you to help you create your list. Take your "sin list" to God in prayer, confessing and repenting before his throne of grace.

Friends

Julie needed a female friend to walk her through this process. We found this friend in her local church. There is no better context on God's earth for restoring a soul than the local church. Just as the hospital is for the physically hurting, so the local church is for the spiritually hurting.

Thankfully, Julie had a friend who was willing and able to help her.

Who is the friend you can talk to? Go to him or her and ask for help. Again, the best place to accomplish this long-term relationship help is in your local church. You may need to ask your pastor for advice with this.

Discipleship

Julie did not need counseling as much as she needed discipleship in the context of the local church. She needed to be taught how to listen and practically apply God's Word to her life on a daily, weekly, and monthly basis. She found a small group that her friend attended and they began to work on the issues at hand. In time, Bob began to participate in the small group as well, though to date he has not been as willing to change at the level at which Julie is responding to God.

The Scriptures make it clear that we cannot grow in our relationship with Christ without ongoing relationships with other believers. Here are a few texts that communicate a body-to-body-type ministry:

▶ "I myself am satisfied about you, my brothers, that you yourselves are full of goodness, filled with all knowledge and able to instruct one another" (Romans 15:14). This tells us that we can all instruct one another.

▶ "And let us consider how to stir up one another to love and good works, not neglecting to meet together, as is the habit of some, but encouraging one another, and all the more as you see the Day drawing near" (Hebrews 10:24–25). This encourages us to stir one another up to do good works.

▶ "Brothers, if anyone is caught in any transgression, you who are spiritual should restore him in a spirit of gentleness. Keep watch on yourself, lest you too be tempted" (Galatians 6:1). This encourages us to serve one another through difficulty.

▶ "If your brother sins against you, go and tell him his fault, between you and him alone. If he listens to you, you have gained your brother. But if he does not listen ..." (Matthew 18:15–16; read up to verse 20). This passage gives us a template for assisting others through difficulty.

Prayer

Going to the Father was one of Julie's most powerful and resourceful helps as we fought for her marriage. God is her best Friend and number one Ally. Therefore, I encouraged her to talk to God often. Julie responded to my counsel and it has had a noticeable effect on her life. I encourage you to follow her example.

Reconciliation

Julie asked God to give her an opportunity to build a bridge to her husband: to befriend him, love him, pursue him, be patient with him. Like the prodigal son in Luke 15, he also needed to repent, but Julie needed to extend biblical love toward him. My approach to Julie was different from my approach to Bob because she was ready to change but he was not.

The following template, based on the Parable of the Prodigal Son in Luke 15:11–17, is a helpful way to think about and respond to those who are unwilling to change. This template was part of my counsel to Julie as I prepared her for the long process of winning her husband in the way that 1 Peter 3:1–6 teaches.

Note the progression, verse by verse, in Luke 15:

▶ Verse 11: We learn about the father with two sons.

▶ Verse 12: The prodigal son asks his dad for his inheritance so he can run away from home and live a self-centered life.

▶ Verse 13: He leaves home and begins a hedonistic spending spree.

▶ Verse 14: He won't listen and his degradation continues. (We see a similar downward spiral in Romans 1:18–32.)

▶ Verse 15: He is living for self. Though things are falling apart, he persists in this lifestyle.

▶ Verse 16: We begin to wonder how long he will stick to his stubborn ways.

▶ Verse 17: The light comes on and *he comes to his senses.* He is now in his right mind; he repents.

It was at verse 17 that the prodigal was ready and willing to change. Let's suppose you meet and begin to talk with him about his sin in verse 13, as I did in an analogous way with Bob. We know from the story that the prodigal is not going to change until verse 17, but you can begin engaging him about change in verse 13. While you understand from 2 Timothy 2:24–26 that repentance is a gift from God, you must patiently wait on God as you serve your spouse. In the meantime you can model for your spouse the behavior you would like to see from him or her.

Personal Application Projects

You will need some blank note sheets, or pages in your journal, to respond to the following questions in a way that will prove most beneficial.

1. If your spouse is a believer, God will finish what he began when he regenerated your spouse (Philippians 1:6). Which are you more aware of: (1) the fact that God will finish what he began, or (2) the problems at hand? Why is this an important question?

2. Repentance is a gift from God (2 Timothy 2:24–26). Do you become impatient, angry, frustrated, or bitter when your spouse does not change, or are you generally trusting in God to bring change to your spouse? Write out how *you* need to change according to this question.

3. Who do you consider to be the bigger sinner in your marriage? You or your spouse? Read

Matthew 7:3–5 and 1 Timothy 1:15 before you
answer. Why is this an important distinction to
make? Write out your answer.

4. Sanctification is a process. In what specific ways
do you need to change in order to keep in step
with what God is doing in your life? Do you
tend to be passive, doing nothing? Do you tend
to be impatient, forcing the issue? Or do you
generally keep in step with God's Spirit?

5. Faith in God and his activity in your life brings
rest to your soul. What are some good things
you recently observed about your spouse and
your marriage that would seem to mean that
God is at work in your life? Start a "gratitude
list" and each day add to this list.

6. Ask your spouse which he or she is most
aware of: (1) your faith that God is working
out his plan; or (2) your fear that things will
never change.

7. Ask your spouse which he or she is more aware
of: (1) your general gratitude for him or her; or
(2) your general displeasure with him or her.

8. How much time do you spend daily in private prayer for your spouse? When you do pray for your spouse, in what specific ways do you express gratitude to God for him or her?

9. A general rule of thumb is that the ratio of your expressions of gratitude to those of displeasure should be about 7 to 1. You should be communicating to your spouse gratitude, thanksgiving, pleasure, and encouragement at a higher rate than criticism. How are you doing with this? How do you need to change?

10. Name two specific areas where it took you many years to change, grow, and mature. Name two specific areas where you need to change, but have not changed yet. Are you tempted to expect your spouse to change today when it has taken you many years to change or, in some cases, you still have not changed? How should you respond to God and your spouse regarding this question?

Where Can I Get Further Help?

Gospel Resources

Mahaney, C. J., *Living the Cross-Centered Life: Keeping the Gospel the Main Thing* (Sisters, OR: Multnomah, 2006)

Vincent, Milton, *A Gospel Primer For Christians: Learning to See the Glories of God's Love* (Bemidji, MN: Focus, 2008)

Marriage Resources

Harvey, Dave, *When Sinners Say "I Do": Discovering the Power of the Gospel for Marriage* (Wapwallopen, PA: Shepherd, 2007)

Ricucci, Gary and Betsy, *Love That Lasts: When Marriage Meets Grace* (Wheaton, IL: Crossway, 2006)

The Counseling Solutions Group, Inc: www.competentcounseling.com

Books in the Help! series include ...

Help! Someone I Love Has Cancer (Howard)
  ISBN 978-1-84625-217-4

Help! My Baby Has Died (Weems)
  ISBN 978-1-84625-215-0

Help! My Spouse Has Been Unfaithful (Summers)
  ISBN 978-1-84625-220-4

Help! I Have Breast Cancer (Frields)
  ISBN 978-1-84625-216-7

Help! My Marriage Has Grown Cold (Thomas)
  ISBN 978-1-84625-219-8

Help! He's Struggling with Pornography (Croft)
  ISBN 978-1-84625-218-1

Help! My Toddler Rules the House (Tautges)
  ISBN 978-1-84625-221-1

Help! Someone I Love Has Been Abused
(Newheiser)
  ISBN 978-1-84625-222-8

(More titles in preparation)